The Handy Credit Repair Handbook

$$ \$\,\$\,\$\,\$\,\$\,\$\,\$ $$

by Gary L. Morris

Table of Contents

NOTES

Notes

What is a Credit Score?

A credit score is a number that summarizes your credit risk, based on a snapshot of your credit report at a particular point in time. A credit score helps lenders evaluate your credit report and estimate your credit worthiness. They use credit scores in conjunction with other pieces of information about you and their own in-house parameters to make decisions about whether to give you the credit that you seek.

Different Types Of Credit Score Models

All lending institutions have put together their own proprietary set of criteria required by borrowers to qualify for different levels of credit. Although these criteria are not considered a credit score but rather an "underwriting policy," the formulas used in these policies are similar to credit scoring models.

The lenders also use consumer credit scores to supplement their underwriting policies in making credit decisions. The FICO credit scoring system is so named because it was developed by the Fair Isaacs Company, and has been the benchmark of credit scoring for almost 25 years; currently over 90% of the top banks and lending institutions use this system.

Your credit reports generated by the consumer reporting bureaus, TransUnion, Experian and Equifax are analyzed using the FICO scoring model to create a 3 digit numeric outcome. The FICO score ranges from 300 to 850.

Note: In order for a FICO credit score to be generated you must have at least 1 credit account on your credit report that is at least 6 months old or better, and there has to be at least 1 transaction during that period noted on the report. So if you do not have any credit at all in the form of a credit card, department store, or gas card then a credit score cannot be calculated.

Another credit scoring model emerged in March of 2006 when the credit bureaus mentioned previously got together and decided that they wanted to develop a generic scoring system of their own known. This system is now known as the Vantage scoring system, and it was an attempt to establish a more consistent rating system between all 3 bureaus. The Vantage scores range between 501 and 990.

To date this system has not been embraced by most of the lending institutions and only 10% of all credit approvals during the year come from the use of Vantage scores. As you are now aware, the information displayed on the credit reports generated by individual bureaus is segregated into different categories according to their particular criteria. So even in a perfect world you could receive 3 different FICO scores because of these reporting differences. Later in this guide we will show or try to show how these 2 scoring systems are similar yet very different.

Reasons Why Credit Scores Are Important To Lenders

Before the use of credit scoring the process of granting credit was very slow, inconsistent and unfairly biased. Back in 1956 Fair Isaac was the first company to develop what we know today as the FICO credit score. This credit scoring system is the most widely used of all the scoring models in effect today, used by 90 of the top 100 lenders to help determine a borrower's credit worthiness.

About 25 years ago the FICO score model was made available to the 3 credit reporting bureaus we know as TransUnion, Experian and Equifax. It was several years later that consumers were allowed to request copies of their FICO credit scores.

Credit scoring has made big improvements possible in the credit process because people can get loans approved faster. Credit scores can be delivered almost instantaneously, helping lenders speed up loan approvals. This means that when you apply for credit, you'll get an answer more quickly. Today many credit decisions can be made within minutes, or online, within seconds. Even a mortgage application can be approved in hours instead of weeks for borrowers who score above a lender's "score cutoff." Credit scoring also allows retail stores, internet sites and other lenders to make "instant credit" decisions.

Using credit Scores, lenders can focus only on the facts related to credit risk, rather than their personal opinions or biases. Factors like your gender, race, religion, nationality, and marital status are not considered in a credit scoring system. In fact it is illegal to use any of the above criteria in credit reports or in credit scoring systems according to the Fair Credit Reporting Act.

Lenders may look at information besides credit scores such as the amount of debt you can reasonably handle given your income, your employment history, and you're the length of your credit history. Based on their review of this information, as well as their specific decision making policies, lenders may extend credit to you although your credit Score is low, or decline your request for credit although your credit Score is high.

How Your FICO Score Is Calculated

The Basis of Your FICO® Score is your credit report whether it is from TransUnion, Equifax or Experian.

Your report details your credit history as it has been transmitted to the credit reporting agency by lenders who have extended credit to you. Your credit report lists what types of credit you use, the length of time your accounts have been open, and whether you've paid your bills on time. It tells lenders how much credit you've used and whether you're seeking new sources of credit. It gives lenders a broader view of your credit history than do other data sources.

Your credit report contains several pieces of information that reveal many aspects of your borrowing activities. The ability to quickly, fairly, and consistently consider all this information, including the relationships between different types of data, is what makes credit scoring so useful.

The FICO® Score is calculated from several different pieces of credit data in your credit report. This data is grouped into five categories as outlined below. These percentages are based on the importance of the five categories for the general population. For particular groups—for example, people who have not been using credit long—the relative importance of these categories may be different.

The percentages in the list reflect how important each of the categories is in determining how your FICO Score is calculated.

Your FICO Score considers both positive and negative information in your credit report. Late payments will lower your FICO Score, but establishing or re-establishing a good track record of making payments on time will raise your score.

- Payment History (35%)

The first thing any lender wants to know is whether you've paid past credit accounts on time. This is one of the most important factors in a FICO® Score.

- Amounts Owed (30%)

Having credit accounts and owing money on them does not necessarily mean you are a high-risk borrower with a low FICO® Score.

- Length of Credit History (15%)

In general, a longer credit history will increase your FICO® Score. However, even people who haven't been using credit long may have a high FICO Score, depending on how the rest of the credit report looks.

- Types of Credit In Use (10%)

The score will consider your mix of credit cards, retail accounts, installment loans, finance company accounts, and mortgage loans.

- New Credit (10%)

Research shows that opening several credit accounts in a short period of time represents a greater risk - especially for people who don't have a long credit history.

On the following pages each of these FICO score components will be discussed in detail.

Personal information on your credit report such as your name and addresses and social security number are only there to identify you. These factors are not used in calculating your FICO® Score.

The importance of these categories will vary for each individual. For example, people who have used credit for very long will be factored differently than those with a longer credit history. The weight of any one factor in your credit score calculation depends on the overall information in your credit report. For some people, one factor may have a larger impact than it would for someone with a much different credit history.

In addition, as the information in your credit report changes, so does the importance of any factor in determining your FICO® Score.

Therefore, it's impossible to measure the exact impact of a single factor in how your credit score is calculated without looking at your entire report. Even the levels of importance shown above are generalized, and will be different for each credit profile.

Components of Your Fico Credit Score

1. Payment History

The payment history extracted from your credit report accounts for 35% of your FICO credit score.

The first thing any lender wants to know is whether you've paid past credit accounts on time. This is one of the most important factors in a FICO® Score.

A few late payments are not an automatic "score killer." An overall good credit picture can outweigh one or two instances of late credit card or auto loan payments.

However, having no late payments in your credit report doesn't mean you'll get a "perfect score." Your payment history is just one piece of information used in calculating your FICO Score.

Account types considered for payment history include:

- Credit cards (Visa, MasterCard, American Express, Discover, etc.)
- Retail accounts (credit from stores where you shop, like department store credit cards)
- Installment loans (loans where you make regular payments, like car loans)
- Finance company accounts
- Mortgage loans

Other items on your credit report are considered when looking at payment history such as collection issues and situations that are a matter of public record.

These types of events are considered quite serious, although older accounts and items with small amounts will count less than recently opened accounts or those with larger balances.

Some of these negative factors include:

- Bankruptcies that will stay on your credit report for 7-10 years, depending on the type
- Home foreclosures
- Lawsuits involving credit accounts, all other lawsuits that involve a criminal offense not related to credit issues cannot be entered on a credit report by law.
- Wage attachments that may have resulted from nonpayment of taxes
- Tax liens on some of your property as well

Judgments

When analyzing the items that have a negative influence on your credit report, the following things are taken into account when determining what your FICO score will be.

The FICO® Score considers:

- How late the payments were
- What was the amount of the delinquency
- How recently they occurred
- How many there are

On a positive note, showing no late payments on accounts on your credit report will help to offset some of the negative items. A good track record on most of your credit accounts will increase your FICO® Score.

2. Length Of Credit History

Length of credit history is evaluated when calculating your FICO credit score and is worth 15% of the score outcome.

In general, a longer credit history will increase your FICO® Score. However, even people who haven't been using credit long may have a high FICO Score, depending on how the rest of the credit report looks. Remember your score is a snapshot of your whole credit picture and even though you may have some weak spots, the final result is that your FICO score may not suffer much.

The following factors are taken into consideration when evaluating the length of time that credit accounts are open.

- How long your credit accounts have been established, including the age of your oldest account, the age of your newest account and an average age of all your accounts
- How long specific credit accounts have been established
- How long it has been since you used certain accounts

3. Types Of Credit IN USE BY YOU

Only 10% of your FICO score is attributed to the types of credit in use by you.

The score will consider your mix of credit cards, retail accounts, installment loans, finance company accounts, and mortgage loans.

It's not necessary to have one of each, and it's not a good idea to open credit accounts you don't intend to use.

The credit mix usually won't be a key factor in determining your FICO Score—but it will be more important if your credit report does not have a lot of other information on which to base a calculation.

The minimum requirement for a FICO score to be generated is that there has to be at least one credit account opened for at least 6 months. Not only that - there must have been some activity in that account during that same 6 month period otherwise FICO has no credit history to assess.

Having credit cards and installment loans with a good payment history will raise your FICO Score. People with no credit cards tend to be viewed as a higher risk than people who have managed credit cards responsibly.

FICO as part of its calculation asks, do you have experience with both revolving credit and installment types of accounts, or has your credit experience been limited to only one account category?Your FICO® Score also looks at the total number of accounts you have. How many is too many will vary depending on your overall credit picture.

Closing an account doesn't make it disappear off your credit report. A closed account will still show up on your credit report, and its history will be considered by your FICO Score.

4. New Credit

New credit accounts on your credit report has a 10% bearing on the final FICO credit score generated. Research shows that opening several credit accounts in a short period of time represents a greater risk - especially for people who don't have a long credit history.

People tend to have more credit today and shop for new credit more frequently than ever. The FICO® Score reflects this reality.

Your Score looks at how many new accounts you have by type of account. It also may look at how many of your total number of accounts are new accounts.

If you have been managing credit for a short time, don't open a lot of new accounts too rapidly.

New accounts will lower your average account age, which will have a larger effect on your FICO® Score if you don't have a lot of other credit information to consider. Even if you have used credit for a long time, opening a new account can still lower your Score.

The score calculation also looks at the inquiries section of your credit report. An inquiry is when a lender makes a request for your credit report or score. Inquiries remain on your credit report for two years, although the FICO® Score only considers inquiries from the last 12 months. The FICO Score has been carefully designed to count only those inquiries that truly impact credit risk, as not all inquiries are related to credit risk.

If you access your credit report it will not be recorded in the inquiries section of your credit report and will not be involved in any score calculation.

There are 3 important facts about inquiries to note:

- Inquiries usually have a small impact in the long run on FICO scores
- Many types of inquiries are ignored completely such as those made by companies evaluating your credit worthiness when deciding to offer you a credit account. An example of such an offer might be that you have been preapproved for our no fee credit card.
- The score allows for "rate shopping." When shopping for any type of credit, whether it is a credit card or a home mortgage, confine your search into a short period of time 2 to 3 weeks in duration. If you do so then these inquiries will count as one inquiry according to FICO.

The FICO® Score may consider the time that has passed since you opened a new credit account, for specific types of accounts. If you have a recent good credit history, late payment behavior in the past can be overcome, re-establishing credit and making payments on time will raise a FICO® Score.

What Is A Vantage Credit Score?

When most people talk about credit scores, they're referring to the FICO score, the brand mostly used by lenders. But, that's not the only credit score out there. Up until 2006 the credit bureaus used scores modeled after the Fair Isaac FICO credit scoring system.

The big 3 credit reporting bureaus Experian, Equifax, and TransUnion had to pay Fair Isaac to license their proprietary FICO scoring algorithm. And being that FICO is the gold standard for lending/credit decisions, it's not like they had a lot of choice... pay FICO or else.

So the 3 credit agencies decided to get together and create their own credit score model, the Vantage Score, without the help of Fair Isaac. As a result the Vantage Score was launched by the three major credit bureaus Equifax, Experian and TransUnion in March 2006 and they released an updated version in October 2010. The credit bureaus came up with the Vantage Score so that consumer credit scores would be consistent among all three credit bureaus.The score range is 501 to 990, and in addition, a letter grade is assigned to each level which is similar to the grading system used in elementary school.

"A" 901–990

"B" 801–900

"C" 701–800

"D" 601–700

"F" 501–600

The Vantage Score is calculated based on the information in your credit report, but the most recent 24-months of credit history have the most significant impact on a Vantage Score.

The score is based on six different pieces of information. The calculation has been updated to give more weight to recent credit and less weight toward your current balances, depth of credit, and available credit.

- 28% Payment history: Whether your payments are satisfactory, delinquent, or derogatory

- 23% Utilization: The amount of credit you've used

- 9% Balances: The amounts owed on recently reported current and delinquent accounts
- 8% Depth of credit: The length of your credit history and types of accounts you have
- 30% Recent credit: The number of recently opened credit accounts and credit inquiries

- 2% Available credit: The amount of available credit on your credit card accounts

You can check your Vantage score without changing your credit status since this type of inquiry doesn't affect your overall credit standing. Your Vantage Score is impacted by inquiries that result from your application for a loan, credit card, or other service.

Since your creditors report different information to TransUnion, Equifax and Experian, the Vantage scores derived from these reports will be different. In some cases creditors will report to only 2 out of 3 credit bureaus, leasing to inconsistency of account information.

The Vantage credit scoring system does not consider:

- Race
- Religion
- Nationality
- Sex
- Marital status
- Age
- Salary, occupation, title, employer, employment history
- Where you live

A Comparison Of The FICO And Vantage Credit Scoring Systems

The Vantage credit score is a world apart from the FICO score. Make sure you know their similarities and most important of all their differences.

How Long Has Each Credit Scoring System Been In Use?

FICO-25 years

Vantage-6 years

What Percentage Of The Top Lenders Are Using Each Scoring System To Help Evaluate A Borrower's Credit Worthiness?

FICO - 90 out of the top lending institutions use FICO exclusively

Vantage - less than 10% of all loans processed in the United States used Vantage as their snapshot of a potential borrower's credit history.

NOTE: For individuals with a less than perfect credit history or those who are rebuilding their damaged credit, using the Vantage credit scoring system would make them more eligible for loans in the "subprime" categories. Subprime lenders are those banks and financial institutions dedicated to borrowers with less than perfect scores or harder to substantiate credit.

Of course these loans would carry a much higher interest rate than those who would normally qualify for a much lower rate because of their good credit standing.

Are The Score Ranges The Same Or Different For Each System?

FICO score ranges from 300-850

Vantage scores range from 501 to 990 and a letter grade is assigned to each level as follows:

"A" 901-990

"B" 801-900

"C" 701-800

"D" 601-700

"F" 501-600

The nice thing about this range is that it's clean and easier to understand. By utilizing a 501 to 990 scale which corresponds to letter grades, even a novice will grasp its meaning.

On the other hand, FICO does not have a neat breakdown by category like that. However for a ballpark comparison, some forums relying on feedback from consumers out there will consider the following to be a fair representation.

- People with a FICO score of 770-850 would be excellent credit risks
- A FICO credit score of 730-769 would be a great credit range and probably would be good enough to secure a loan with a decent interest rate
- A FICO score range of 700-729 would be good credit but probably would not qualify you for some of the best credit cards out there

- A FICO score range of 640-699 would be considered as fair credit but even on the upper end of that range would probably not qualify you for many credit card opportunities

- A FICO score range of 581-639 represents a bad credit rating and would designate you as a high risk borrower. Some unsecured department store or gas cards may be available to those at this level. You might have to investigate using a "secured" credit card.

- Finally a person with a FICO score range of 300-580 is an extremely bad credit risk and a "secured" credit card may be your only option for credit card approval. Later in this book we discuss "secured" and "unsecured" credit cards.

Are The Formulas The Same For Calculating Their Scores?

The formulas for both FICO and Vantage scores are secret, so no one can tell you exactly how they are calculated. However both companies do provide some basic information as to the general categories and how they affect your score.

The Vantage Score formula uses 6 components, versus the FICO formula which consists of 5. What you need to keep in mind though is that each major component consists of several sub-components (of which the percentages for each aren't publicly available). An apple to apples comparison of these components is not really possible as is shown in this following example.

According to FICO's website, the "Amount Owed" category consists of:

- Number of accounts with balances

- Amount owed on accounts

- Amount owed on specific account types

- Proportion of credit lines used

- Proportion of installment debt which is owed

- Lack of a specific type of balance, in some cases

Those 6 sub-components, when combined, equal 30% of your credit score.

On the other hand, Vantage Score doesn't have an "Amounts Owed" category but judging from their category names, one can make an educated guess that they still look at those 6 sub-components. The difference is that it appears they aren't all grouped under the same mother category, making an apple to apples comparison very difficult.

You can use this rough approximation to estimate your FICO rate based on your Vantage score. Keep in mind that this is just to give you a very rough estimate.

So for an estimate, you can multiply your Vantage score by 0.86 to give you an idea of what neighborhood your FICO score would be in.

EXAMPLE: If your Vantage Score was 851, you would multiply that by 0.86 and the number you would get back is around 732 – an estimation of your FICO score.

Conversely if you wanted to see what your Vantage score would be if your FICO score was 732, you would multiply 732 by 1.14 and the result would be around 835. As you can see the formula is not exact in reverse but it does let you know that the result is a solid "B" under the Vantage scoring system.

What Are Some Of The Identifiable Differences Which Affect The Final Score Calculation In Both FICO And Vantage Scoring Methods?

FICO weighs payment history more heavily than Vantage does.

EXAMPLE: A person who has a long 20 year credit history with only 1 open account that has had no activity for the past 5 years could have a high Vantage score in the 800s and a lower score under FICO because consistent activity on that person's accounts over time has less weight under the Vantage scoring system. It is apparent that Vantage gives much less weight to current balances than does FICO.

- FICO seems to more heavily favor having a diverse mix of both installment loans and revolving credit (i.e. credit cards). Yet some consumers say that they had only 1 of these types of accounts and still had a high Vantage score.

- Vantage seems to take into account your credit limit on accounts instead of just the debt-to-credit ratio which is the amount of debt that you have on an account divided by the total limit on the account.

EXAMPLE: A person with accounts with high credit limits and substantial balances may have a higher Vantage score and would rate much lower under the FICO system which considers debt-to-credit ratios more stringently.

What's The Bottom Line?

Of course we all want the best, but what is the highest possible credit score, the 850 for FICO or 990 for Vantage is almost unattainable. In fact, there are many loan officers that have been in the business for years who have said they've never seen a perfect credit score before. Furthermore, you can have a FICO score in the high 700's and it will usually get you the best rates anyway.

Ultimately, instead of focusing on reaching the highest credit score possible, concentrate your efforts on having:

- A good mix of credit (revolving accounts like credit cards as well as installment accounts, like mortgages, student loans, or car loans)

- Keep your credit utilization on revolving accounts low (no more than 30% of your limit, but ideally, under 10%)

- The older the accounts, the better! If you have an old credit card you hate, don't cancel it. Keep it open and use it occasionally since that account may be helpful for your score given its age. However if the card has an annual fee and you're not using it, then usually it does make sense to cancel it.

The Only Way To Request Your Real FICO Credit Score

Remember that the FICO credit score is used by over 90% of the nation's lending institutions and has been for over 25 years.

The credit scores that you can purchase from the 3 credit bureaus TransUnion, Equifax and Experian are Vantage credit scores and they are there for you to consider but you should use them as an educational tool rather than rely on them too heavily as a barometer of what you can expect to hear from lenders regarding your credit worthiness.

Purchasing your FICO credit score will be a much more reliable tool to use when considering making a big ticket purchase.

You cannot purchase a FICO score based on your Experian credit report anymore but accessing your score from both TransUnion and Equifax should give you a very good idea of your credit worthiness.

The only way to request your FICO credit score is online.

Go to www.myfico.com. From the home page click on "check my FICO score"

Next page, under products at a glance click on "FICO Standard"

Next page click "get my fico score now" and you will be directed to a shopping cart page with different options. Make sure that you select the correct package.

During the purchase process you will be asked to give personal information such as your name, address, social security number, and date of birth so that your identity can be verified and your credit report can be accessed from the credit bureau.

When you finish your purchase you will automatically be able to review your product online for a 30-day period. If you have any questions about your product or have trouble gaining access to your product then call 1-800-319-4433.

This is what you will receive when you choose FICO Standard

The TransUnion package will cost $19.95 and separately the Equifax package will cost $19.95 also.

In each package you will receive:

- Your credit report
- Your FICO credit score
- A full explanation on the positive and negative factors affecting your score
- Access to the FICO Score Simulator which will show you how your FICO score will change when you do any of the following:

- Pay your bills on time for many months

- Miss a payment

- Pay down your debt balances right away or monthly

- "Max out" your credit cards

- Get a new mortgage, auto loan, credit card

- Get instant credit at a department store

- Transfer balances to a new credit card

- Declare bankruptcy

Requesting Your Vantage Credit Score From The Credit Bureaus

The only way that you can receive your credit score is by first having secured a copy of your credit report from the credit bureau where you are now applying.

To access your Free credit report from each of the 3 credit bureaus, TransUnion, Equifax and Experian which you are entitled to once every 12 months, visit annualcreditreport.com and follow the prompts. If you need further help then we offer a step-by-step set of guides to help you through the process. Go to the Table of Contents under Section 1 and select your preferred method of accessing your credit report-online, by phone or by mail.

TransUnion

Online Access

When you receive your FREE TransUnion credit report through the annual credit report portal, you will be offered a chance to buy your Vantage credit score which you will have to pay for. Online the cost is $9.95, see a lesser expensive option below by ordering by phone or mail.

Order By Phone

To request your Vantage score provided by TransUnion call 1-800-916-8800 and press "3" to speak to a customer representative. You must have your credit report file number handy and be able to provide personal information such as name, address, social security number and date of birth so that your identity can be authenticated. The fee for your Vantage credit score is $7.95.

By Mail

You need to provide the following information if requesting your TransUnion Vantage credit score by mail:

- File number on your TransUnion credit report
- Full name and mailing address
- Last four digits of your social security number
- Description of your request, which is, that you are requesting your TransUnion Vantage credit score.

Make your check or money order payable to TransUnion for $7.95. If you are paying by credit card then provide the following, card type, account number and expiration date. It is strongly advised for security reasons that you do not pay for a transaction through the mail using a credit card, though it is still an option.

Mail your request to:

TransUnion

P.O. Box 1000

Chester, PA 19022

Equifax

Equifax has a money saving deal that will provide a copy of all 3 credit reports from Equifax, Experian, and TransUnion along with Vantage credit scores from each bureau for a flat fee of $16.95. If each credit score were purchased separately it would cost around $7.95 per copy. Some states are offering a discount but that discount is not available through Equifax. This offer is only available by phone or online.

Order Online

Go to www.Equifax.com and select Equifax Advantage Plan for $16.95 which includes the 3 credit reports and credit scores from each credit bureau.

Ordering By Phone

Call: 1-800-846-5279 and you will be connected to a customer representative who will assist you in buying this 3 bureau credit score package for $16.95. It will be delivered to you by email or by the postal service.

If you just want your Equifax credit score then you will pay $7.95.

Be prepared to provide personal information such as your name, social security number, and date of birth so that your identity can be authenticated.

Ordering Process By Mail

The offer listed above is not available by mail. You can only receive an extra Equifax credit report by mail for $11.00 and your Equifax Vantage credit score for $7.95. It will be delivered in 7 to 10 days.

The following information must be included with your request:

- A copy of 2 valid picture IDs such as a driver's license, state ID or a military ID
- Check or money order made out to Equifax for 11.00 for the credit report mentioned above and $7.95 for the credit score both from Equifax only.

Mail your request to:

EQUIFAX
P.O. Box 740241
Atlanta, GA 30374

Experian

Online Access

Read this very carefully.

You can access your Experian Vantage credit score online for $1.00 but to get this rate you have to enroll in Experian Credit tracker. You can grab your credit report and score within the 7 day trial period and run and if you don't cancel by the 7th day you will be charged $17.95 for a month's service which includes a bunch of information that you may or may not want. This offer is not available to New York residents.

Order By Phone

Call: 1-888-397-3742 and Press "2" on your key pad. Next press "1" which asks if you want to purchase a credit report or score. Then press "2" which asks if you want to purchase your credit score. Finally select "1" to pay by credit card.

The fee for an Experian Vantage credit score report is $7.95 plus applicable tax

By Mail

The following information must be sent to request your Experian Vantage credit score:

- Full name including initial if applicable
- Current mailing address as well as all other addresses where you lived in the past 2 years
- Date of birth and social security number
- A copy of either a driver's license, state ID or military ID card
- Copy of 1 utility bill, bank or insurance statement which shows clearly your full name, current address and date issued

They will not accept credit card statements, voided checks, lease agreements, magazine subscriptions, or postal service forwarding orders as proof.

Enclose a check or money order for $7.95 plus tax payable to Experian

Mail request to:

Experian
P.O. Box 2002
Allen, TX 75013

The report will be sent in 10 business days or less.

15 Issues That Can Hurt Your Credit Score

The following issues are the most influential components used in calculating your credit score.

- **Paying Late:**

35% of your score is payment history. Consistently being late on your credit card or loan payments will lower your credit score.

- **Not Paying At All:**

Completely ignoring your monthly payments on credit cards, installment loans such as car loans and mortgage payments is far worse than being late on these obligations. In the instance of a credit card nonpayment, each month that no payment is made moves you closer to having the credit card account charged off.

- **Having An Account Charged Off:**

When creditors think you're not going to pay your credit card bills at all, they charge off your account. This account status is one of the worst things for your credit score.

- **Having An Account Sent To Collections:**

Creditors often use third-party debt collectors to try to collect payment from you. Creditors might send your account to collections before or after charging it off. A collection status shows that the creditor gave up trying to get payment from you and hired someone else to do it.

- **Defaulting On A Loan:**

Loan defaults are similar to credit card charge-offs. A default shows that you have not fulfilled your payment requirements set forth in the loan contract that you signed.

- **Filing Bankruptcy:**

Bankruptcy will devastate your credit score and will stay on your record usually for a period up to 10 years. Every recourse should be considered before finally taking this action. Seeking the advice of a consumer credit counselor would be in your best interest.

- **Having Your Home Foreclosed:**

Getting behind on your mortgage payments will lead your lender to foreclose on your home. In turn, the late payments will hurt your credit score and make it harder to get approved for future mortgage loans.

- **Getting A Judgment Against You:**

A judgment shows you not only avoided your bills, the court had to get involved to make you pay the debt. While they both hurt your credit score, a paid judgment is better than an unpaid one. So if possible try to make some type of payment arrangements with the courts and the hit on your credit score will be far more temporary than not attempting to pay the judgment at all.

- **Keeping High Credit Card Balances:**

The second most important part of your credit score is the level of debt measured by credit utilization. Credit utilization is the amount of credit that you have actually used in comparison to the total amount of credit that is available to you on a specific account.

Example: For every high balance that you carry on your credit card accounts will increase credit utilization and make you less credit worthy.

Your credit score will be lowered as a result. It is felt that because your balances are high that you are more of a credit risk than those who keep their balances under 30% of the total credit limit. If possible balances should be kept even lower than 30% to achieve maximum credit scoring consideration in this category.

- **Maxed Out Credit Cards:**

Maxed out and over-the-limit credit card balances make your credit utilization 100%. This status will reflect badly against your credit score.

- **Closing Credit Cards that Still Have Balances:**

When you close a credit card that still has a balance, your credit limit drops to $0.00 while your balance remains the same. This makes it look like you've maxed out your credit card, causing your score to drop.

- **Closing Old Credit Cards:**

Another component of your credit score, 15%, is the length of your credit history, longer credit histories are better. Closing old credit cards, especially your oldest card, makes your credit history seem shorter than it really is.

- **Closing Credit Cards With available Credit:**

If you have several credit cards some with balances and some without, closing those credit cards without balances increases your credit utilization.

Example: In total your available credit on all credit cards is $10,000. You have open balances of $2000 on all accounts so your utilization percentage is 20% which is good. Now consider that you decide to close credit card accounts that you have not used which have a total limit of $5000 making your total credit limit on all accounts reduced to $5000. Your new credit utilization ratio is 40% which is on the high side when calculating your credit score.

- **Applying For Several Credit Cards Or Loans:**

Credit inquiries account for 10% of your credit score. Making several credit or loan applications within a short period of time will cause your credit score to drop. Keep applications to a minimum.

- **Having Only Credit Cards Or Only Loans:**

Mix of credit is 10% of your credit. When you have only one type of credit account, either loans or credit cards, your credit score could be affected. This factor mostly comes into play when you don't have much other credit information in your credit history.

Disputing Errors On Credit Reports

Reasons To Correct Errors On Your Credit Report

When looking at your credit report, whether it is from Experian, Equifax or TransUnion, you owe it to yourself to examine every line in the report for accuracy. These reports are your financial picture and are viewed by creditors, banks or other loan institutions, potential employers, and others who need to assess your credit worthiness.

Credit Report Errors Can Include The Following:

- Something you did not buy or authorize
- Amounts that differ from that which you actually paid
- Different dates listed on your payments and obligations that you do not concur with
- Items not properly identified
- Math errors
- Missing payments that you made on your obligations
- Accounts attributed to you that do not belong to you
- Application requests listed that you never filled out

The following items on your credit report should be scrutinized carefully to make sure that the information shown is clear and accurate. Some of these items will not be applicable to everyone.

- Credit accounts including revolving accounts like credit cards
- Installment accounts such as auto loans
- Mortgages
- Student loans and personal loans
- Bankruptcies

- Collections
- Liens
- Judgments
- Inquiries
- Personal identification information including name, social security number, address, current employment etc.

Equifax Credit Report Dispute Process

Before Getting Started

We suggest have a current copy of your personal Equifax credit report handy.

If you have not requested a copy of your Equifax credit report in over "1 year" then go to annualcreditreport.com and follow the process to access your credit report.

There are three different methods for initiating an Equifax credit report dispute.

- By phone
- By mail
- Online with Equifax

Register Dispute By Phone

For those of you who are not comfortable navigating the internet, you can still get your Equifax credit report corrected and know that all the information on the report is true and accurate.

Step 1: Gather all the questionable items together before you call.

Step 2: Make sure you have the confirmation number which is a 10 digit number located at the top of your credit report along with personal identification information such as your social security number and date of birth.

Note: If your copy of the Equifax credit report does not have a confirmation number listed then you must select "Stop Here" to register your dispute by mail or online.

Step 3: Call Equifax Dial 1-800-685-1111.

A customer representative will assist you and determine if you can proceed with your dispute by phone. Certain corrections need backup documents to prove the need to make changes to the credit report. For instance if your social security number is wrong or your address is listed incorrectly then a copy of your driver's license or a copy of a utility bill may have to be sent to Equifax. You will be given full instructions if this situation happens.

Sending Your Credit Report Dispute By Mail

Step 1: Make sure that you have noted your personal information such as name and address, social security number and date of birth.

Step 2: For each correction requested label the incorrect version on your credit report as "Old" and the corrected information as "Updated." If you are unsure whether supporting documents need to be sent to Equifax to back up your reasons for requesting corrections to be made, then call the number listed above and a representative will guide you in this matter.

Step 3: Send your packet to Equifax by a method that can be tracked such as Express Mail or Priority Mail to:

Equifax Information Services LLC
PO Box 740256
Atlanta, GA 30384

Initiating Your Equifax Credit Report Dispute Online

If you are not sure if your Equifax credit report is recent enough, once online at Equifax.com go through the verification process to establish whether the report is new enough.

If it is too old, even if you requested your free report within the one year period, you will have to purchase a copy of your Equifax report before you can continue.

Step 1: Make note of the areas of your Equifax credit report that you feel is incorrect.

Step 2: Go to Equifax.com and click on "online dispute."

Step 3: On the next screen under "What would you like to do?" Click "get started."

Once your dispute is submitted, in a month or so you can come back to the site and repeat step 2 and on step 3, then click on "check your status."

Step 4: Follow the verification process so that Equifax can find your file.

Step 5: Select the area of your report where the incorrect information that you are disputing can be found. You may select more than one section of the report and there are links to review that which you have indicated as being incorrect information. You will be able to review and change or edit the areas of dispute before submitting your request.

Step 6: When you are satisfied that all your disputed items have been selected then submit your dispute. You will be notified by email in most cases within 30 days of submission. Some corrections take up to 45 days to fix. At that point you will be given a corrected Equifax credit report.

It is strongly advised that you should go through the process of analyzing and correcting the other 2 credit reports from Experian and TransUnion. Eventually that which you had corrected on your Equifax credit report will for the most part be noted on these other credit reports. Don't take the chance that this will automatically happen; file separate disputes for each credit report.

Filing Your TransUnion Credit Report Dispute Online

Step 1: Make sure that you have all the corrections you want to address on your credit report, ready to enter once online.

Step 2: Go to www.disputetransunion.com You must log-in or create an account to enter any dispute request.

Once logged-in you will be asked to provide your email address, this info may already be entered in the box. Next you will have to check "4" boxes to certify that you are not a machine and that you are only viewing your own credit report.

The next screen wants you to enter for security purposes some more personal information, your name, social security number, and current zip code.

General Instructions For Reviewing Each Section Of Your Report

- Each section will have a "help" clickable link to offer specific assistance in determining how to indicate that which is incorrect in that section.
- After each item in each section click the "update" or "investigate" button to indicate that there are errors pertaining to that line item.
- When finished reviewing all suspect items click "continue" to see a review of all entries in your dispute request. Your dispute is not complete untilyou click "submit" to send the transmittal to TransUnion.

Helping You To Complete Your Dispute Successfully

Credit Report Section By Section Special Notes

Personal Information

There are no special notes for this section.

Account Information

Typically account information is updated monthly but for every account the date of last update will be shown on the report.

Adverse Accounts

Most accounts listed here will remain on your credit record for 7 years from the date of the first delinquency. Account numbers may be partially encrypted or scrambled and this is normal to protect your privacy.

Satisfactory Accounts

Accounts in this section have been reported to have no adverse information, and as above, all account numbers are either partially encrypted or scrambled.

Promotional Inquiries

All companies listed here have received "only" your name, address and other limited information in order to make an offer of credit or insurance. These inquiries are only seen by you and do not change your credit score.

Account Review Inquiries

The companies in this section obtained your credit report in connection with a pending application, account review or other business transactions with you. These inquiries are only seen by you and do not change your credit score.

Consumer Statement

Be careful to only enter a statement that you want to be seen by all creditors for a period of 2 years, of course the consumer statement can be deleted by you at any time. This statement should be a general comment about a life situation that is creating adverse problems with your credit.

Examples:

- "Bankruptcy due to medical bills"
- "Delinquency due to divorce proceedings"

You can make an entry if you have been unemployed for a long period of time, but if you only had that status for 6 months then refrain from making a statement about this and just notify a creditor directly if necessary.

Disputing Information On Your TransUnion Credit Report By Phone Or Mail

Request Investigation By Phone

Be sure to have all the corrections that you wish to have made on your TransUnion credit report ready before calling for help in processing. In addition have your file number ready as well as your social security number and date of birth in case requested by the representative.

Call: 1-800-916-8800 and select option "3" to speak to a representative. You will be guided through the steps needed to complete your report dispute request.

Request Investigation By Mail

Step 1: Personal Information

You must provide the following personal information for TransUnion to locate your file.

- Full name and file identification number which should be located at the top of your credit report. If you do not have a file number, TransUnion will be able to locate your information with the other personal data required. If more than one name is indicated on your credit report then make note of them also.
- Current address and telephone numbers where you can be reached in case of questions
- Employer's name and address, if you are not employed at the moment just write "Not employed at present"

- Social security number, if this field on your credit report is encrypted and only the last four digits are visible then enter your SSN
- Date of birth
- Driver's license number, if you do not have a driver's license then enter "Do not have a driver's license"

Step 2: Enter Investigation Details

For each incorrect item provide the following information as stated on your credit report:

- Company name and account number
- Enter "This information is inaccurate because:"

You must choose one of the following reasons why you are disputing the information on this account.

- This is not my account
- I have never paid late
- This account is in bankruptcy
- This account is closed
- I have paid this account in full
- I paid this before it went to collection or before it was charged off
- Other:

If you choose "Other" then give specific information.

Step 3: If information regarding previous address or employment is incorrect; first show the incorrect data and then indicate how the information is to be changed to reflect a more accurate representation of the details in this category.

Step 4: Signature

Please do not forget to sign and date your request, as your submission will be returned to you without a signature.

Step 5: Mail Your Request

It would be a good idea to send this request by secured mail as you are submitting sensitive material. Use either Priority or Express Mail for example.

Send request to:

TransUnion Consumer Solutions

P.O. Box 2000

Chester, PA 19022-2000

What Happens After I Submit My Dispute Request?

TransUnion will contact the lender in question or the public record source to start the investigation asking them to verify the information that you are providing.

The company will return their findings to TransUnion within 30 days or at most 45 days depending on the disputed items. TransUnion will then send you a corrected copy of your credit report. If the item in question cannot be verified by TransUnion, in some cases it will be deleted from your report.

Submitting An Experian Credit Report Dispute

Before Getting Started

You must have a current copy of your personal Experian credit report handy.

Don't Have A Current Copy Of Your Experian Credit Report?

If you have not requested a copy of your Experian credit report in over "1 year" then go to www.annualcreditreport.com and follow the process to access your credit report.

If, on the other hand you have already received your free copy allotted to you in a 12 month period then visit Experian.com and you will have to pay for a copy.

There are three different methods for initiating an Experian credit report dispute:

- By phone
- By mail
- Online with Experian

Submit Dispute By Phone

Your Experian credit report must have a report number at the top of the document to use this service, if not "Stop Here" and review the ways that you can obtain the report that you need by following the instructions in the above section "before you start."

Gary L. Morris

The only sections of your report that you can dispute by phone are potentially negative accounts, accounts in good standing and personal information. Before you call make sure that you have your report number and the partial account number of the items in question and any of the specific entries in the personal information section that are incorrect.

If ready then dial 1-800-493-1058 and then enter your report number. Follow the automated system prompts to enter your dispute.

Unfortunately Experian does not have a live customer service representative that can assist you with this process so you might feel more comfortable requesting your dispute by mail or online.

Submit Your Dispute By Mail

You do not have to have an Experian credit report that has a report number to use this service. The following information must be sent to Experian to initiate your dispute.

Report number if available, your full name, address, the account name, and partial account number of the item being disputed and why the item is being disputed. Do not include your social security number or date of birth unless you do not have a credit report number to furnish.

Send your transmittal to:

Experian
P.O. Box 9701
Allen, TX 75013

To Initiate Your Dispute Online

Step 1: Go to www.Experian.com/review report and enter your report number which is located at the top of your Experian credit report. If your report does not have a report number, "Stop Here," you cannot file a dispute online. Your only option is to send in your request by mail. Should you still want to file a dispute online then an Experian credit report with a report number must be obtained to continue with this online process.

- Select the state where you live and enter your social security number
- You must check the 3 certification boxes that say that you are only accessing your own credit report and you are not a machine.

Click "submit"

Step 2: Select the area of your credit report where the incorrect information can be found. If you need to visit more than one area then you can return to this page and select another section to edit.

These are the sections of your report that you can have corrected:

- Potentially negative items
- Accounts in good standing
- Personal information
- Your personal statement

Step 3: Once you have selected the section of the report that you want to visit, choose the account that you want to dispute by clicking on the account name and a new page will appear.

Step 4: Click on "dispute this item" and a new screen will appear. If you are in either of these two sections, "Potentially negative items" or "Accounts in good standing," you will see a combo box where you must choose the best reason as to why you are disputing the information on the account you have selected. Only one choice may be selected for each account disputed.

Here are the choices in the combo box:

- No knowledge of account
- Account paid in full
- Account closed
- Unauthorized charges
- Belongs to "X" spouse
- Balance incorrect
- Included in bankruptcy
- Belongs to primary account holder
- Corporate account

Step 5: There is an "additional information" box where you can enter up to 120 characters of text to further explain the selection from the combo box in step 4. It is not a box for entering another reason for disputing that particular account.

Don't forget to click "submit dispute" before you move on to addressing another account or to dispute either personal information or make a personal statement. You can also choose to click "cancel" if you change your mind about disputing that item.

Step 6: You can dispute any information listed in the "personal information" section by simply selecting an item, clicking on that item, then answering the question that applies to that particular item.

Step 7: If you want to enter a "personal statement" which is a general explanation of why your credit report may not look very favorable to lenders, then click on that category and you will choose the best statement that fits your situation.

I Have Documents To Send That Support My Reasons For One Or More Of My Disputes, What Do I Do?

If you have a court or legal document, a letter or other piece of evidence to support your dispute request, then send it to the address listed at the top of this guide under "By Mail." Be sure to include your full name, report number, address and account and partial account number listed for the account in question. Do not send your social security number or date of birth, the report number will allow Experian to retrieve that information.

Why a Credit Score Still Means Something at 50+

There are many consumers of fifty years of age and over whose credit scores have been damaged in recent years by the fickle financial climate. On average however, those of us who are over 50 still have better credit scores than many. As we head into our retirement years though, it's possible to become a little complacent about our credit ratings. We are debt free and not interested in borrowing any more, so what's the big deal if our credit score "ain't what it used to be?" Well, the truth is, it does matter, and for some very specific reasons you may not have thought of.

We Should Still Be Diligent About Identity Theft

Though great measures have been incorporated into our society in order to prevent identity theft, it still occurs. The fact is, as vendors and lenders implement strategies to combat identity theft, thieves exert as much energy into figuring out how to get around them. Almost 10% of American households have at least one member who has fallen victim to this heinous crime, which continues to increase. (US Bureau of Justice)

Monitoring our credit reports and credit scores on a regular basis is an effective means of protecting ourselves against identity theft. If we check our credit report regularly there is a greater chance of catching any abnormal transactions before they can do much harm. Look for any new accounts that you did not open, credit card transactions, even loan applications that are not of your doing. Even an increase in the number of inquiries can expose fraudsters trying to open accounts in your name.

The Possibility of Medical Emergencies

As we get older there is a greater chance of us becoming ill. Maintaining a healthy credit score will ensure that we can get the loan we need if saddled with huge medical expenses. Many accounts that are in collection are there because of unpaid medical bills, in fact it is one of the most common reasons for debt. Our insurance may not cover everything, and it is comforting to know that the funds we may need for ourselves or our loved ones will be available if we need them.

Take Advantage of Better Insurance Rates

Many of us who are over 50 still need to pay auto and home insurance. There is a 2:1 chance that our insurer uses our credit score in determining how much they charge us and what discounts we qualify for. The higher our credit score is, the better our chance of receiving the best possible rates, savings we can put towards our retirement and the amenities we'd like to go with it!

Better Employment Opportunities

Unfortunately many people over 50 have been forced to return to work in recent years. Anyone in that position needs every advantage they can get, and a good credit score is an ace to have up your sleeve. Many employers factor an applicants credit score into their decision making progress of who to hire. They feel a good credit score is an indication of responsibility and reliability. Though they need your permission to view it, refusing them access could lead them to believe you have something to hide, even if that's not true. Consequently your chances of securing a senior position, or employment in general, could be jeopardized.

Though we may be over 50, it doesn't pay to be complacent about something that affects so many different areas of our lives. Paying attention to our credit scores can save us embarrassment, hardship, and most of all, money!

Getting to Grips With Your Client's Credit Score

It's quite possible that you have not yet had the need to talk to any of your clients about their credit score, but that could change down the road. Credit scores are coming more to the fore as the financial crunch hits, and the future could see you holding some awkward conversations. The status of a person's credit score must be approached carefully and clinically. Someone with a bad credit score could be easily offended by the approach or choice of words.

Clients may feel embarrassed by a broker asking if the carrier can consider their credit score to determine their rates, and that could be especially difficult if they have never had to do so before. The number of carriers that consider credit scores is growing daily; it may be wise for brokers and customer service reps to reconsider their individual business practices.

Mind the Customer's Needs

Industry insiders are increasingly stressing the importance of minding the customer's needs. This includes having a clear understanding of what credit scores are yourself. Though some say that credit scores shouldn't be used by carriers, others consider them to be a good tool for assessing risk. Regardless of your personal views on the subject, the needs of the client must be put first. A good place to begin is with a discussion about cost versus coverage. Though credit scores do impact the cost of a policy, they are not the only factor to consider, even in the current "credit score climate." Stressing this to a client will help put their mind at easy about discussing the matter.

If there is no need to breech the subject, then of course discretion is the better part of valor. Not all carriers consult credit scores, so if you can get them the best price from one that doesn't, the point is pretty much moot. That doesn't mean you shouldn't ask the carrier what prompts their quotes, as factoring the client's credit score into the process might result in even greater discounts.

Have a Handle on Credit

There may come a time when you have to deal with credit scores on a regular basis. Understanding how credit score work and what effects them can help you to give your client better service. Credit bureaus factor in a bunch of things in calculating a person's credit score, but basically they are bill payment history (35%), the amount they currently owe (30%), the length of their credit history (15%), the types of credit they use (10%), and new credit or recent credit applications (10%). Encourage clients to also educate themselves about their credit scores and to take steps to raise them so that they can secure better rates.

The easiest way to avoid the issue is to consider only carriers that don't use credit scores. To tell a client their rate has been affected by their credit score is one thing; to tell them that but then follow up with alternative options is another. Prepare yourself to dodge their anger however, you should be prepared to tell them that you didn't know their credit score would be a factor. Keep in mind that although the rules of disclosure may be in place, not every insurer adheres to them. Though you may never have to discuss a credit score with a client, it is best to be prepared to do so knowledgeably if you must. It will help you to gain the trust and respect of clients, which can only lead to a better and mutually beneficial relationship in the long term.

Really? Save Money and Improve My Credit Score Using Store Credit Cards?

Everyone knows that store credit cards have a great rewards system, but not many are aware of how using them responsibly can help you to save even more money. That might seem preposterous considering the interests rates attached to them, but responsible spending and timely payments can help you to avoid incurring any interest charges at all.

Store credit card holders save lots of cash by taking advantage of the discounts and special sales days that their issuer offers them. They save money on their purchases, often get free shipping for the items they buy, and frequently receive cash bonuses for just signing up. If you strategize your applications and spending you can consistently raise your credit score, which can save you even more cash. To understand how that works you need to know a bit about how a credit score is calculated, so, let me briefly explain.

How Raising Your Credit Score Can Save You Cash

One third of your credit score is calculated according to your payment history. In other words, if you have consistently paid you bills and made your loan and credit card payments on time throughout the course of your life, you will most likely have a higher than average credit score. On the other hand, if you have regularly missed paying bills, or made late payments to credit cards and loans, your credit score will most likely be on the low side.

The key to using a store credit card to raise your credit score is to charge only small amounts every month and pay your balance off in full before the grace period expires. This will save you money in several ways. First, you will not be subjected to any interest payments, as interest is only charged to your balance. A zero balance equals zero interest charges. Secondly, you will not have to pay any late fees or penalties. Thirdly, and this could save you tens of thousands of dollars in the future, it will help to raise your credit score. A word of warning however – don't apply for too many credit cards at once, as this will affect your credit score negatively.

People with higher credit scores receive lower interest rates when applying for loans, and get a better APR on their credit cards. Because they are not considered as high a risk as consumers with low credit scores, lenders are more eager to attract their business, and consequently make it less expensive for them to pay borrowed money back. Imagine the savings over the course of a 30 year mortgage just by receiving an interest rate of one percentage point less.

The key to saving money by using a store credit card, or any credit card for that matter, is responsible and clever spending and payment. Charge little; pay a lot, and your credit score will increase consistently over a relatively short period of time. If you plan to apply for a loan at some point in the future, you should acquire a credit card and begin using it as soon as possible to develop your credit history.

If you follow the above strategy for several years, by the time you apply for your loan or mortgage, not only will lenders say yes, but they will thank you for your business by giving you a better rate.

Don't Let Your Student Loan Sabotage Your Credit Score

For many, the process of applying for, securing, and then paying off a student loan is their first step into the world of money management. How you handle your student loan could sabotage you financially for a long time after graduation if you are not careful. When you first apply for credit, your credit history begins. It will be consulted throughout your lifetime in calculating your credit score. A high credit score will see you able to secure a loan or mortgage with little difficulty, and at prime rates. A low credit score however could see you having a difficult financial time in the future, unable to secure a loan, mortgage, or even a credit card.

One of the greatest negative effects on an individual's credit score is a failure to pay bills on time, or defaulting on loan or credit card payments. Your bill payment history makes up a massive 35% of your credit score. If you continually make late payments on your student loan or miss them completely, it can seriously affect your credit rating. As you miss payments the amount you owe will increase due to accumulated interest. The amount you owe at any time makes up another 30% of your credit score. As you can see, you can control 65% of your credit score simply by paying bills and making loan payments on time.

How your credit history unfolds is completely in your hands. You can shape your credit history and build a healthy credit rating by being financially responsible. It might be difficult, and you may have to make huge sacrifices, but doing so could save you from serious trouble or financial strain in the future. If you are struggling to make regular payments on your student loan, the sooner you take action to correct that the better.

What to Do if You are Struggling to Pay Your Student Loan

If you are having problems making your student loan payments there are several steps you can take to prevent it sabotaging your credit score. The first thing you should do is contact your loan provider as soon as possible and alert them to the situation. You may be able to arrange a new payment plan that is easier to meet on a monthly basis by extending the repayment period. You may also qualify for forbearance, deferment, or loan consolidation. Deferment and forbearance allow you to postpone or reduce your payments in order to help you avoid defaulting.

During a deferment you are excused from making payments on the principal or interest for a set period, and in some cases, depending on the type of loan you have, the government will even pay the interest (Direct Subsidized Loan, Federal Perkins Loan, or Subsidized Federal Stafford Loan). If you have unsubsidized loans you will have to pay the interest, but not until the deferment period is over. Keep in mind however, that interest will continue to accrue during the deferment period. Ask your loan provider or organization that handles your loan if you qualify.

A forbearance may be granted to you if you can't make your payments but don't qualify for a deferment. A forbearance will give you relief from monthly payments for up to one year, but interest will continue to accrue on both subsidizes and unsubsidized loans. There are two types of forbearance, mandatory and discretionary. A discretionary forbearance may be granted on the discretion of your lender due to illness or financial hardship. Your lender must grant you a mandatory forbearance if you qualify.

Taking action now to avoid defaulting on your student loan can save you from financial hardship and future disappointments. Working with your lender to avoid defaulting on your student loans bow will ensure that you can borrow money in the future when you're ready to buy a house or car. Educate yourself further about deferments, loan consolidation, and forbearance so that your student loan doesn't sabotage your credit score.

Improve Your Credit Score and Bank on a Better Mortgage Rate

One constant that remains throughout the ever-changing financial and economic landscape is the importance and benefits of a good credit score. One of those great benefits of a healthy credit rating is securing a mortgage at better rates than average. If you plan to apply for or take out a mortgage, you can save thousands of dollars by making sure your credit score is in the best shape it can be, and by understanding the role a credit score plays in the loan application and lending process.

When a person secures a loan they are obligated to pay interest on the money borrowed. That is common knowledge, but few realize how the interest rate that they are charged is determined. Determining that interest rate depends largely on three particular criteria; the size of the loan (amount borrowed), term of the loan (amount of time given to repay), and the applicant's credit score. Because of the importance of the credit score in the lending process, it is critical to understanding how it is calculated.

How Credit Scores are Calculated

The largest single determining factor in calculating a person's credit score is their history of bill payment. Your payment history makes up a whopping 35% of your credit score. The first time you open a credit-related account, your bill payment history begins. If at any time after that you miss a payment or worse let an account go into collections, that action is reported to the credit bureaus. A history of missed or late payments will practically guarantee you a low credit score, making it difficult for you to secure future credit. The reverse is also true however, and if you have consistently paid bills on time you most likely have an above average credit score.

The amount you owe at any one time makes up another 30% of your credit rating, while the types of credit you take out, any new credit you may have recently been granted, and the length of your credit history make up the remaining factors. If you don't know it you should check your credit score as soon as possible. You can find information on how to receive a copy of your credit report and get your credit score from one of the major credit reporting agencies – Equifax, Experian, or TransUnion.

How Your Credit Score Saves You Money on a Mortgage

The Fair Isaac Corporation (FICO), the company that developed the credit score rating system, monitors the interest rates given to borrowers over the course of time and uses that data to determine an estimate of interest rates for specific ranges of credit scores. The most recent figures available indicate quite a difference between consumers with above average credit scores and those with scores on the low side.

The credit score range is 350 – 800. An above average credit score is considered to be one that above 760. Few people have perfect credit scores of 800, and not many have scores below 500. Generally credit scores fall in the 580-720 range. Within that range however, there can be vast differences in the interest rates attached to mortgages. According to the FICO scale, the interest rate given to mortgage applicants with credit scores in the 680-699 range is approximately 3.5%. If your score is just 40 points or so different however, you could pay nearly 1.5% more interest on your mortgage. That is quite a difference if you figure out the savings over the course of a 30 year mortgage. A loan amount of $250,000 at a fixed rate of 5% over 30 years with monthly payments of $1342.05 will end up costing $483,139.46. That's a total of $233,139.46 interest paid.

If you have a credit score that entitles you to a rate of 3.5%, your monthly payments on a mortgage at the same terms would be $1,122.61 (saving you over $200 per month), the end cost would be $404,140.22. That's almost $80,000 saved on interest just by having a credit score of 680 instead of 630.

As you can see from the above figures, a good credit score can save you a healthy chunk of cash on your mortgage. You don't have to have a perfect score (although it wouldn't hurt!), but, if you can improve your score up to the 680 mark or above, you'll be in a great position to secure those prime interest rates.

How to Build a Credit Score Quickly

Besides having a bad credit score, something that can make it difficult to get credit is having no credit history. You can't get credit without a credit history, and you can only develop a credit history by taking out credit. There are simple ways to establish a credit history and steps you can take to build a credit score fast. One of the most effective methods of developing a credit history for those with none is to take out a secured credit card.

Use a Secured Credit Card to Build a Credit Record

For many of a young age who have not had a chance to establish any kind of credit record, a secured credit card is an excellent option. You can open a secured card account by depositing an amount with your bank. The bank will then issue you a card with a line of credit equal to the amount you have deposited. The money you deposit is usually held as a security against the money you are "loaned" (the limit of your card). If you deposit $1,000 for instance, you will be issued a card with a limit of $1,000.

A secured card works exactly like a credit card, you can shop online with it, book airline and hotel reservations, and anything else you can do with a normal credit card. A long as you don't go over your limit and make your payments on time, you will be on your way to establishing a good credit score. Normally after one year, if you have not breeched the terms and conditions of your secured card, your initial deposit will be released and your secured card becomes a standard credit card.

Other banks have a system where after 12 months of responsibly handling a secured card, you can apply for a normal credit card. Generally, if you have handled the secured card well, your application for a standard credit card will be granted.

Handle Your Secured Credit Card Responsibly

Even though you will have deposited an amount of money to secure the line of credit issued to you on your card, late or missed payments and exceeding your card's limit will be penalized. Your bill payment history makes up 35% of your credit score, so making payments on time is crucial to establishing a good credit score.

If you can, only charge amounts that you can pay off completely every month. This will not only go a long way to building an excellent credit rating, but will protect you from having to pay any interest on your charges. If you cannot pay the complete balance of your card off, try to keep it to below 30% of your card's limit. According to the credit bureaus, maintaining such a balance shows that you handle credit intelligently, and your credit score is rewarded accordingly.

Building a credit score is no harder than simply opening a secured credit card account and managing it responsibly. After having a secured card for a year, apply for a small personal loan, or ask for a credit increase to your card. Make sure you don't take any more than you can comfortably pay however, as remember, missed payments hurt your credit score the most. Constant payments made on time however, can help you to build a healthy credit score in no time.

Build a Better Credit Score for Your Small Business

Having a good credit score is imperative for any small business owner. Creditors simply won't lend money to people they deem unlikely to pay it back. A good credit score lets the financial world know that you and your business are reliable and can be trusted to repay loans and other bills. Establishing a stellar credit history doesn't happen overnight, but there are some simple measures that can be taken to show that your business is creditworthy.

Separate Your Personal and Business Accounts

An effective way to protect the creditworthiness of your business is to set up accounts in your company name. It's easier to get a loan if your business is an established one with an address on file and a record of paying its bills each month rather than if you are a freelancer working out of your house. Lenders will take your business more seriously if it has its own identity. Even if your personal credit score or credit history is less than admirable, establishing a record of positive business transactions improves the creditworthiness of your business. Keep your personal and business accounts separate, and maintain a good record of company payments. Showing that your business pays it bills and debts on time shows that it is a good candidate for funding.

Another effective tool for building a good credit score is a company credit card. This can help you to quickly establish a credit history for your business. As an added bonus you can rack up points to be used for prizes and rebates while you are building a credit record. As long as you pay your statement on time every month your credit score will increase accordingly. A good practice is to maintain a balance of less than 30% of your card's limit. This shows that your business is not entirely dependent on credit.

Build a Better Personal Credit Score

As the owner of a small business; your personal credit score will reflect the creditworthiness of your business until it can establish a history of its own. A good personal credit score will help you to gain easier access to capital, build trust with those you do business with such as banks or vendors, and most importantly show that you are a good credit risk.

Some things you can do to improve your personal credit score are:

- Know what your credit score is and understand how it is calculated.

- Obtain a major credit card such as MasterCard or Visa and pay it off regularly.

- Use credit only when you really need it. Borrow a small amount that you can pay off quickly and easily and your credit score will improve dramatically. Not using credit at all will hurt your credit score, as it will reduce your credit history, which makes up 35% of your credit rating.

- Pay your bills on time and even pay in advance when you can. Some vendors may give discounts for up-front payments. If you are able to make advance payments you can lower your operating costs and improve your cash flow at the same time. This prevents black marks on your credit report for late payments and lowers the cost of your inventory.

Banks and other creditors take a risk when they provide you with capital. It is therefore important to make your goals and how you plan to reach them very clear. As your company moves from the start-up to growth stage, you may very well need additional funding, and lenders want to be sure that you are not a bad credit risk. Pay your bills on time and build a solid credit history so that financing is available when you and your business need it.

Don't Let Divorce Destroy Your Credit Score

Although divorce proceedings won't affect your credit score directly, the financial issues entangled in the process may. Often these issues involve joint accounts, and each party is answerable for the actions associated with them. It is extremely important to deal with such accounts prior to the divorce if you are listed as an authorized user, co-signer, or joint owner. The best option is to close the accounts completely, but at least ensure that your name is removed from them. A credit report is filed for each individual associated with a joint account for any actions taken on it, so the irresponsible act of one partner could hurt the credit rating of the other.

The role of the divorce decree confuses many divorcing couples. Although a divorce decree might specify which individual is responsible for particular accounts opened during the marriage, it doesn't nullify the contract with creditors. If the spouse designated as responsible in the divorce decree is unwilling or unable to pay, and there has been no change to the contract by the lender, late payments will appear on the credit reports of both individuals. This will impact the credit scores of both parties in a negative way, and though missed payments may occur after the divorce is final, they will still be reported for each individual associated with that account.

Vindictive behaviour by one or both spouses during a divorce is often responsible for damage to credit scores. It has been the case in the past that an angry spouse has sought to hurt the other by charging large amounts on credit accounts, either to intentionally wreck their credit score, or just to punish them. In either case the result is the same, unfortunately the offending party often overlooks the fact that they are damaging their own credit rating at the same time.

Separate Your Credit From That of Your Spouse

It is best to separate your credit history from that of your spouse as soon as possible. The earlier you can do so in the divorce proceedings the better off you both will be. This is much easier to do if you can both remain civil during the process, as creditors will need to be contacted with a request to alter the existing contracts. Ask them to remove you as a joint owner or authorized user. The lender may require that one of you be designated as responsible for the account, though that is not always possible.

If you cannot be removed from the account and can't afford to continue payments, request that no further charges be allowed on it. This will at least keep you from accumulating more debt, and you can resume payments when you can afford them. Most lenders understand the divorce process and what is involved and are happy to work with individuals to clear debt. If you don't qualify for a personal credit card account, ask your spouse to let you assume responsibility for an existing one. At least this way you can continue to use it and develop your own credit history.

It might be difficult to work with your spouse to ensure that you continue to pay joint debts during the divorce proceedings. Working with each other to close existing accounts and to pay off outstanding debt however is the best approach to take. Doing so will enable you both to make a clean break, and leave the financial burdens that could haunt you both post-divorce behind. There is no reason why either partner should allow divorce to destroy their credit score.

How to Use Your Inheritance Loan or Cash Advance to Improve Your Credit Score

Yes, you read right! Your inheritance loan or cash advance can be used to improve your credit score rather than lowering it. So you ask, how can taking on more credit improve my credit score? The answer is actually quite simple, though you should know and understand a bit about inheritance loans and cash advances first. Many people think they are the same thing, or don't realize that they even exist. Either one can be used to raise your credit score, but you must first understand the difference before deciding which one is for you.

What is an Inheritance Cash Advance?

If you are due to inherit money or property that is currently in probate, you can get an inheritance cash advance. An investor will simply purchase your inheritance claims for a lump sum cash payment up front. The investor then becomes the "heir" to your inheritance. The monies you receive are not considered a loan; there are no monthly payments or interest you will need to pay. Once you receive the cash, the deal is done. Even if after probate it is found that there is no money left over to pay the investor, you are not liable. That is a chance that the investor takes. An additional benefit is that your credit score is not a factor in whether you receive a cash advance or not.

What is an Inheritance Loan?

You may be able to secure a personal loan from a traditional lender based on the worth of an inheritance, but you will still need a good credit score, and things such as your employment history and job status will be taken into consideration. An inheritance loan taken out with an institute such as Heir Advance Company is more of an assignment than a personal loan. In exchange for all or a portion of your inheritance, you can receive an advance up front to help with current expenses. One of the greatest advantages of an inheritance loan is that you can use it to improve your credit score.

The Strategy

Because there are no monthly payments to make, no interest, and no up-front costs involved in securing an inheritance loan with Heir Advance Company, the full sum can be used in a specific way to raise your credit score. Depending on the size of your advance or loan, you can put a lump sum aside especially to be used to clear overdue or over-the-limit accounts. Don't close those accounts once you clear them though, as doing so will diminish your credit history. This will have the opposite affect of lowering your credit score. Keep those accounts open, but don't max them out in the future, and use your inheritance loan to pay more than the minimum whenever you can.

If you have lots of outstanding and overdue bills and don't want to pay them completely off at once, formulate a payment plan. A considerable portion of your credit score is made up of your bill payment history. Use the money advanced to you through your inheritance loan or advance to ensure regular payments to those bills. A good way to do so is to set up a specific account and employ standing orders for each bill. This way each bill will be paid on time every month until they are paid off. Your bill payment history will improve, and consequently so will your credit score.

An inheritance loan can provide you with a lump sum of money to help you to get your financial life back on track. If you currently have an inheritance that is in probate, consider an inheritance loan or cash advance. In addition to relieving your financial stress, it can ne used to improve your credit rating, and ensure that you qualify for a traditional loan should you need one in the future.

Warning: Not Understanding Your Credit Report Could Cripple You Financially!

We are all becoming aware of the importance of our credit scores and reports, but do we really understand them? It is important to know your credit score, and equally as important to review your credit report regularly. But what if we don't know what to look for, or don't understand the content of our credit reports? The truth is a lack of understanding of the information in our credit reports can lead to a lack of action. That lack of action could cripple us financially forever. There is no need to panic or become overwhelmed however, as the following information and corresponding plans of action can help you to understand, and repair any errors in your credit report.

The Most Important Aspects of Your Credit Report

Personal Data

The first thing you should do when you receive the copy of your credit report is to make sure your personal information is correct. Your name, birth date, social security number, employer, and current and precious addresses should all be checked and corrected if they are wrong. Wrong information makes identity theft easier, and could even be a sign of identity theft. If there is just one digit wrong in your social security number, someone else's bad financial practices could end up on your credit record, and could affect your credit rating for a very long time.

Number of Inquiries

Inquiries are made every time you apply for credit. Too many inquiries on your credit report could be an indication that you rely too heavily on credit. This will adversely affect your credit score, and consequently make it difficult to acquire credit in the future. Inquiries are listed for a period of two years after which they are deleted. Check the inquiries on your report and make sure it is you who applied for that particular line of credit. If you see any inquiries from lenders with whom you have not made a credit application, contact the reporting agency immediately. This could well be an indication of identity theft.

Accounts Information

All of the lenders with which you have credit will be listed in this section. It will include credit card accounts (including department store cards), loans, and any other accounts that you pay in installments. Each account will be listed as active or delinquent, so make sure that any accounts listed as active actually are. If you have closed or paid off an account and it is still listed as active, contact the creditor immediately and ask that they update your information with the credit bureaus.

The Single Most Important Item in Your Credit Report

In 2012 the Consumer Financial Protection Bureau (CFPB) conducted a study that revealed that an individual's credit card usage is the most important factor in determining their credit score. The CFPB is a consumer watchdog site run by the US Government, designed to enable consumers to file complaints and to provide financial information, advice, and aid. The CFPB accumulated and analyzed data from the three major credit reporting agencies in the country and discovered that "credit card history dominates the information in credit reports."

The three major credit reporting agencies – Experian, TransUnion and Equifax, possess more than 200 million files on consumers across America. Those files are updated on a monthly basis, and more than 50% of those updates are from credit card companies. Keeping your credit card use to a minimum and paying off your balance in full every month can not only save your credit score, it can steadily raise it.

The information contained in your credit report is used to calculate your credit score. Making sure that information is accurate and correct can make all the difference between you receiving that crucial loan and not. Your credit score also determines what interest a lender will charge you. If you haven't done so lately, check your credit report now, and use the above information and guidelines to correct any wrong information that could be crippling you financially.

www.ingramcontent.com/pod-product-compliance
Lightning Source LLC
Chambersburg PA
CBHW070132210526
45170CB00013B/837